THE BEST OF
Indonesian
COOKING

THE BEST OF INDONESIAN COOKING

Published in the United Kingdom by
CENTURION BOOKS LIMITED
52, George Street, London W1H 5RF

British Library Cataloguing in Publication Data
A catalogue record for this book is available from the British Library.

ISBN: 0 948 500 08 5

Photo credits:
Michael Freeman: Cover, pages 1, 4, 14, 20, 25, 27, 31, 32, 36, 37, 39, 42, 48,
51, 52, 54, 59, 62, 69, 70 and 75
Benno Gross: Pages 8, 19, 28, 40, 54, 65, 68 and 80.

Design and Artwork supplied by Centurion Design Forum Ltd.
Printed in Hong Kong by Paramount Printing Co. Ltd.

THE BEST OF
Indonesian
— COOKING —

A selection of popular Indonesian Recipes

SRI OWEN

CENTURION

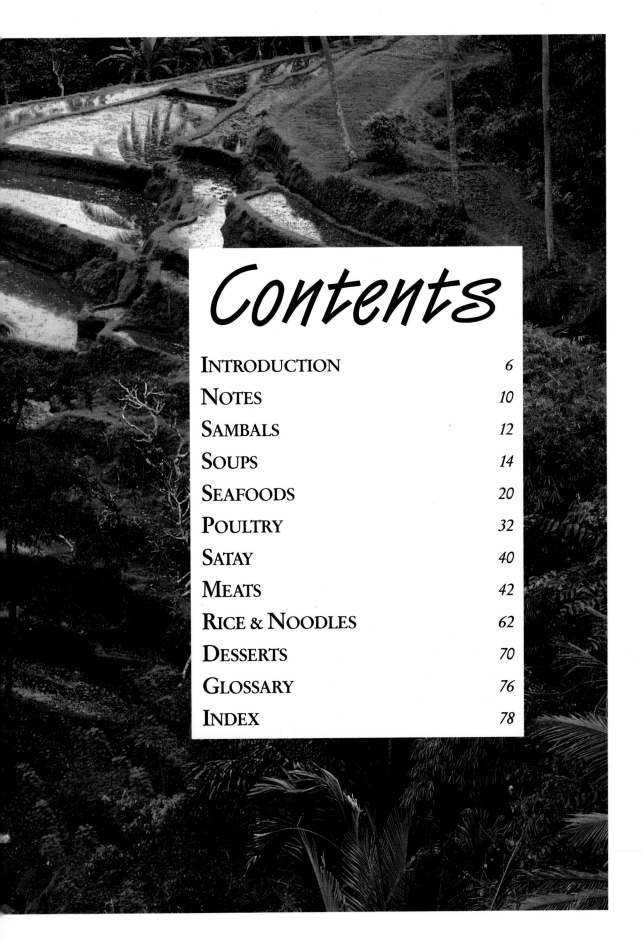

Contents

Introduction

Indonesia can hardly help producing some of the best food in the world. Its countless islands all lie near the Equator, but their variety teems. Some are vast, some tiny; a few barren, but most fertile; monsoons and volcanoes have given each its peculiar character of rainfall and soil. Here, every cook is an explorer.

Indonesians appreciate, respect and love good food, and they do so all the more because poverty and hunger have never been very far from their lives. We never take food for granted. It is necessary for life, so it must be one of the best things in life. It demands care and knowledge, and above all it demands enjoyment.

Our extraordinary history has multiplied the differences among the islands and their people. Parts of Java are as overcrowded as anywhere in the world, while much of Kalimantan is practically empty. We live on what has always been a crossroads of world trade, so for more than two thousand years we have absorbed influences from travellers and conquerors – Indians, Chinese, Arabs, Europeans. We have learnt something from each of them, but never quite forgotten what we knew before. This is as true of agriculture and cooking as it is of religion and politics.

Obviously, our staple food in most of the islands is rice. Everyone, even the very poor, tries to eat rice three times a day, even if all he has with it is a little salted fish and some chilli. We like our food hot and spicy. But this does not mean that Indonesian dishes have to be chilli-hot; just a little chilli will sharpen and point up the flavours of the dish without burning your mouth. We also like a little sourness in our cooking to offset the natural sweetness of many of our ingredients, so you will find tamarind and lemon grass in many of our recipes.

Most Indonesians eat a very healthy diet; some of us may be a little overweight, but obesity is rare. Rice, even when it has been milled and polished, is one of the healthiest and most nourishing grains. We eat a lot of fresh fruit, salads and lightly-cooked vegetables. Coconut oil is, I admit, high in saturated fat, but until very recently we have eaten no dairy products and very little red meat.

A characteristic of traditional Indonesian cooking was that preparation times were often quite long: spices had to be chopped and ground, meat and vegetables had to be cut up small. The chopping and grinding can now be done quickly and easily in a blender or food processor. It is still worth spending time, though, to trim the fat and gristle from meat, and to cut everything into what I refer to as "bite-size pieces". For many dishes, the cooking time is relatively short, everything comes to table fresh and hot, and the food is easy to eat – at home, we eat with spoons or, more traditionally, with our fingers.

Other dishes, it's true, are long-cooking; Rendang is the obvious example. Many have the advantage that they can be cooked well in advance and re-heated. A night or two in the fridge can actually improve the flavour, because it gives the sauce or spices extra time to penetrate. Don't feel that you have to serve an all-Indonesian meal, or even to maintain culinary barriers within a single course. Combining Indonesian dishes with Chinese, French, Italian, or those of any other cuisine, can lead you to create many original and delicious menus.

For this book, a few classic dishes have been adapted from my *Indonesian Food and Cookery* (Prospect Books, London, 1986); the changes that I have made in ingredients and techniques reflect the changes in shopping and eating that are taking place so swiftly, both in Indonesia and in Europe.

FOOD, DRINK AND TABLE MANNERS

My earliest memories are of a traditional household in central Sumatra, where three generations lived under one roof and the kitchen was always busy. I learnt to eat with my parents, sitting at table and using a spoon and fork, but I preferred to be in the big room next to the kitchen and to eat with my fingers. Eating gracefully and tidily this way is not difficult, but it takes a little practice. Remember that only your right hand must touch food. I still find that real Indonesian food tastes best eaten this way, but the next best is a spoon, so you can polish off the rice and the sauce. Indonesians of course do not use chopsticks.

In most houses, all the main-course dishes come to table together and people help themselves. Guests refill their plates as often as they want – the more often you do this, the bigger the compliment to your hostess. You don't have to pile your plate every time or mix everything together. Indeed, it is not polite to overload your plate and leave a lot of food uneaten; we make a point of providing a big spread, but none of the food on display will be wasted.

As children, we were discouraged from drinking anything at mealtimes, on the grounds that it would make us feel bloated. An important part of a traditional Indonesian meal is a large bowl of soup, which stays on the table throughout. You can eat the soup by itself – with a spoon, of course – or with your other food. This is the only liquid people normally take while they eat. However, when I cook in London I serve the meal in separate courses, so the soup, if there is any, comes to table on its own. Indonesians don't drink alcohol, but the belief that Indonesian food is too spicy to be accompanied by wine is wrong – many full-bodied red and white wines go excellently with it. The Dutch drank lager with their rijsttafel, which is also good.

Notes

EQUIPMENT

You do not have to have any exotic pans or tools. However, a blender or food processor is a great help in making the pastes or spice mixtures that we used to grind by hand. A wok is an asset in any kitchen. If you are going to cook rice fairly often, a rice steamer or double saucepan is useful, and if you cook rice more than about twice a week an electric rice cooker, though quite costly, is a good investment.

QUANTITIES

The recipes were written using metric measurements and the Imperial alternatives (bracketed) have been rounded up or down to serve as a practical, rather than a precise, guide. Measurements over 75 grams (75g) or 75 millilitres (75ml) are shown in units of 25 and below that in 5g teaspoons (tsp) or 15g tablespoons (Tbsp).

I use a cup for measuring rice if it is to be boiled or steamed, because then I can measure the water in the same cup – it is volume that matters here, not weight. The basic rule is 1 cup of liquid to 1 cup of rice. If you like your rice very soft, increase the liquid by 1/4 – 1/2 a cup – not more. If the rice is to be fried later, don't increase the liquid, and do give the rice time to cool before frying.

The quantities shown in these recipes will be sufficient for 4-6 people, unless otherwise stated. This assumes that the dish is part of a meal, and that two or three other dishes are served, plus rice. Recipes that demand 1.5 or 2 kilograms (3 – 3½lbs) of meat, or more, will be enough for 8-10 people if they are part of a meal. A chicken or duck cut into halves will feed two people if it is served only with a salad or a cooked vegetable. With rice and another cooked dish, it will be enough for four.

RICE

Indonesians like rice that is fluffy and slightly sticky – the Javanese call this quality *pulen*. Any good-quality long-grain supermarket rice will do perfectly well. Basmati, when cooked, is too dry and firm for Indonesian taste, but that need not stop you using it. In Britain, I usually buy Thai Fragrant rice (also called Jasmine rice) from a Thai shop if I am cooking plain boiled or steamed rice. However, this is fairly expensive and may not be easily obtainable everywhere. "Easy-cook" rice has been parboiled; if you buy this, follow the instructions on the packet. Cooked parboiled rice tastes like "ordinary" rice but is not fluffy or sticky, so most Indonesians would not choose it. Rice noodles are described in the Glossary. Rice flour is used mainly for making sweets and cakes.

COCONUTS

The coconut is almost as important in South-East Asia as rice is. Directions for making coconut milk are given in the Glossary; desiccated coconut is perfectly good for this, but "fresh" coconut is even better and is called for in a few recipes. I put quotation marks round "fresh" because the nuts you buy in Britain are always pretty old, but they are none the worse for that. When buying a coconut, hold it up to your ear and give it a shake. If you can hear water slopping about inside, the nut is probably still good. If there is no liquid in it, the nut may be rotten, so avoid it.

Some violence is needed to get into a coconut. I use a Chinese meat cleaver, but a hammer is just as good. First, detach the flesh from the shell by holding the nut in one hand and tapping it firmly and repeatedly all over with your hammer or the blunt side of the cleaver. Then split the shell by putting the nut on a really solid surface and holding it steady with one hand while you give it a good blow with the cleaver or hammer. It doesn't need a wild, dangerous swing; the shell will soon crack open if you hit it around its waistline, not at the ends.

When the nut cracks the water will run out; if you have a jug handy you may be able to catch most of it. Some people like to drink it, though it tastes of little except sugar and is not used for any of the recipes in this book. When you have prised out the flesh, and before grating it, it is usually necessary to peel off the brown rind with a potato peeler, otherwise the colour will make the dish look unattractive. For coconut milk, however, the rind can be left on; it will not discolour the milk. You can grate the flesh either with a hand grater or by cutting it into chunks and putting these, in batches, into a food processor.

SAMBAL

A sambal is a spicy, sometimes dry but more often moist, relish. The basic ingredient is chillies, but the presence of other spices makes some sambals less fierce than others. You can use sambal in your cooking, but if you are not sure of your guests' or your own reaction to it you may prefer to serve the sambal separately so that everyone can take what they want. Where a dish goes best with a particular sambal, I have mentioned this in the recipe. A name like Sambal Goreng Udang indicates, of course, not a relish but a main-course dish; in this case the sambal is the spice mixture which is made and fried as an integral part of the dish.

Recipes for sambals overleaf.

SAMBAL ULEK
(crushed red chillies with salt)

1 kilo (2¼ lbs) fresh red chillies
1 Tbsp salt
1 Tbsp vinegar
1 tsp sugar
1 Tbsp groundnut oil

Discard the stalks from the chillies, wash and place them in a saucepan. Add sufficient water to cover and bring to the boil. Simmer for 15 minutes, then drain and place in a blender together with the salt, vinegar, sugar, oil and 4 tablespoons of hot water. Blend until smooth, then allow to cool and place in jars with tightly-fitting lids. Store in the refrigerator (up to 2 weeks) until required.

SAMBAL BUBUK TERI
(hot chilli relish with dried anchovies)

450 g (1 lb) dried anchovies
(ikan teri)
150 g (5 fl oz) sunflower oil
3 shallots
3 cloves garlic
1 Tbsp dried chilli flakes

Remove the heads from the anchovies. Slice the shallots finely and chop the garlic. Heat 125 g (4 fl oz) of oil in wok and stir-fry the anchovies, in batches, for 4 minutes, then remove with a slotted spoon into a colander lined with absorbent paper. Leave to cool then use a mortar and pestle and pound to a coarse powder. Heat the remaining oil in a small saucepan and stir-fry the shallot, garlic and chilli flakes for 2-3 minutes, then add the anchovy and stir for a further minute. Remove and drain on absorbent paper before serving.

SAMBAL KECAP
(soy sauce with chillies)

3 small chillies
2 shallots
1 clove garlic
2 tsp fresh lime juice
1 tsp olive oil
1 Tbsp light soy sauce
1 Tbsp dark soy sauce

Remove the seeds from the chillies. Finely chop the chillies, shallots and garlic and mix with the lime juice, olive oil and soy sauce.

Author's Note
This sauce is particularly good with sate, especially for anyone who does not like peanut sauce. It is very easy and quick to prepare, and lovely to dip Chinese or Vietnamese spring rolls into, to spoon lightly over fried noodles, or to serve as a dip for crunchy raw vegetables like carrots and celery.

Sambal Tomat
(tomato sauce)

4 shallots
3 fresh red chillies
25 mm (1 inch) knob fresh ginger
1 tsp crumbled shrimp paste
2 Tbsp sunflower oil
450 g (1 lb) ripe tomatoes
1 tsp sugar
1/2 tsp salt

Slice the shallots. Remove the seeds from the chillies. Finely chop the chillies and ginger. Heat the oil in a wok or saucepan and stir-fry the shallots, ginger and shrimp paste for 1-2 minutes. Add the chillies and stir for a further minute, then add the tomatoes, sugar, salt and 225 ml (8 fl oz) of water. Bring to the boil, then lower the heat and allow to simmer for 10 minutes, or until the tomatoes are well cooked. Finally, mash the tomatoes roughly with the back of a wooden spoon and serve.

Author's Note
In Indonesia we would use the sambal as above but if you like a smoother sauce pass it through a sieve before serving. Like all other sambals, Indonesian tomato sauce is usually chilli-hot, but this version is quite mild. If you like it hotter add more chillies.

Sambal Kacang
(peanut sauce)

225 g (8 oz) raw peanuts
4 shallots
2 cloves garlic
1 tsp crumbled shrimp paste
1/4 tsp salt
125 ml (4 fl oz) vegetable oil
1/2 tsp chilli powder
1/2 tsp brown sugar
1 Tbsp dark soy sauce
1 Tbsp tamarind water

Shell the peanuts. Chop the shallots and garlic and pound in a mortar together with the shrimp paste, salt and 1 tablespoon of water, to produce a smooth paste. Heat the oil in a wok and fry the peanuts for 4 minutes, stirring continuously. Remove with a slotted spoon and leave in a colander to cool, then grind, or pound, to a fine powder. Discard all but 1 tablespoon of oil from the wok, re-heat, and fry the spice-paste for 1 minute. Then add the chilli powder, sugar, soy sauce and 450 ml (16 fl oz) of water. Bring to the boil and stir in the ground peanuts. Cook over a moderate heat, stirring occasionally, for 8-10 minutes until the sauce becomes thick, then add the tamarind water and stir to mix thoroughly.

Author's Note
This popular sauce is most often eaten with sate or gado gado but can also be served as a dip for crudites (in Indonesia, lalab) and other savoury snacks. If not eating immediately allow to cool and transfer to a jar with a tightly-fitting lid. It can then be kept in the refrigerator for about 1 week.

Soups

Soto Ayam
(spicy chicken soup)

1 small chicken
salt
freshly ground black pepper
2 Tbsp dried shrimps
6 shallots
3 cloves garlic
2 candlenuts
3 Tbsp corn oil
1 tsp finely chopped ginger
$1/4$ tsp turmeric powder
$1/2$ tsp chilli powder

Garnish:
75g (3oz) transparent vermicelli
75g (3oz) beansprouts
1 Tbsp chopped spring onion
1 Tbsp chopped flat-leaf parsley
2 Tbsp sambal ulek (see page 12)
4 slices lemon

In a large pan, bring 1.5 litres ($2^1/_2$ pints) of water to the boil. Halve the chicken and add to the pan, together with a little salt and pepper, then lower the heat and allow to simmer until the chicken is cooked, approximately 40 minutes. Strain off the stock and reserve. Cut the chicken meat into small pieces and discard any fat. Reserve the bones. Meanwhile, soak the dried shrimps in warm water for 5 minutes, then drain. Chop the shallots, garlic and candlenuts and place in a blender together with the shrimps and 2 tablespoons of water. Blend for 30 seconds. Heat half the oil in a saucepan and stir-fry the paste for 1 minute, then add the ginger and turmeric and stir well. Add the bones, pour in half the stock, and bring to the boil. Lower the heat and allow to simmer for 15 minutes. Strain into a clean saucepan and add the remaining stock and the chicken. Bring back to a slow boil, adjust seasonings to taste and leave for a further 2-3 minutes, then transfer to a soup tureen and serve with a plate of garnish.

To prepare the garnish soak the vermicelli in hot water for 2 minutes, then drain. Blanch the beansprouts. Arrange all ingredients on a serving plate.

Author's Note
Put the plate of garnish next to the soup tureen with a sufficient number of individual soup bowls. Guests can then help themselves, taking the garnish first and ladling the soto over it.

Sayur Bayem
(spinach soup)

450 g (1 lb) young spinach leaves
125 g (4 oz) sweet potato
2 shallots
1 small green chilli
pinch ground ginger
1 bayleaf
salt to taste

Wash the spinach and chop coarsely. Peel the sweet potato and cut into small cubes. Finely slice the shallots and chilli and place in a saucepan together with the ginger, bayleaf, salt to taste and 450 ml (15 fl oz) of water. Bring to the boil and add the sweet potato, then cover the pan and allow to simmer for 10 minutes. Uncover the pan and add the spinach together with a further 300 ml (10 fl oz) of water. Bring back to the boil and cook for a further 2-3 minutes until the spinach is tender. Finally, adjust seasonings to taste, remove the bayleaf and transfer to a tureen.

Soto Babat
(tripe soup)

2 Tbsp dried shrimps
1 large potato
400 g (14 oz) tripe
salt
1 large onion
3 candlenuts
5 cloves garlic
2 small dried chillies
1.2 litres (2 pints) chicken stock
2 Tbsp peanut oil

Garnish:
3 tsp fried shallots
1 Tbsp chopped spring onions
lemon slices

Soak the dried shrimps in warm water for 30 minutes, then drain and set aside. Peel the potato, slice thinly and place in a bowl of cold water. Put the tripe in a saucepan, add sufficient water to cover and 1/2 a teaspoon of salt. Bring the water to the boil and cook for 35-40 minutes, then drain and cut the tripe into bite-size pieces. Slice the onion and place in a blender, together with the candlenuts, garlic, chillies and 75 ml (3 fl oz) of stock. Blend for a few seconds to a roughly-crushed paste. Put 2 tablespoons of oil in a small saucepan and fry the paste for 3-4 minutes, stirring continuously. Add half the stock and simmer for 10 minutes. In the meantime, pour the remaining stock into another saucepan and bring to the boil. Drain the slices of potato and add to the boiling stock. Cook for 8 minutes, and add the tripe. Strain the liquid from the first pan into the pan containing the tripe and continue to simmer for a further 10 minutes. Finally, transfer to a soup tureen and garnish with the shallots, spring onion and lemon slices.

Sop Buntut
(oxtail soup)

450 g (1 lb) oxtail
2 carrots
2 parsnips
1 onion
4 shallots
4 cloves garlic
salt to taste
10 black peppercorns
2 Tbsp peanut oil
1 tsp finely sliced lemon grass
Pinch ground galingale

Garnish:
1 Tbsp fried shallots
1 Tbsp chopped flat-leaf parsley

Joint the oxtail. Dice the carrots and parsnips and slice the onion, shallots and garlic. Put the oxtail into a large pan together with the carrot, parsnip, onion, salt and peppercorns and cover with 2 litres ($3^1/4$ pints) of water. Bring to the boil and simmer for $1^1/2$ hours, skimming off any scum that comes to the surface. Remove the oxtail with a slotted spoon and cut into smaller pieces. Strain the stock into a bowl and set aside. Heat the oil in a clean saucepan and fry the shallot and garlic for 1-2 minutes, then add the meat and cook for a further 2 minutes, stirring continuously. Pour in the strained stock, together with 600 ml (1 pint) of hot water and bring to the boil, then lower the heat and allow to simmer for 35 minutes. Finally, adjust seasonings to taste and transfer to a soup tureen. Garnish with the fried shallot and chopped parsley and serve immediately.

SOTO DAGING
(spicy beef soup)

450 g (1 lb) brisket
2 Tbsp dried shrimps
6 shallots
2 cloves garlic
20 mm (3/4-inch) knob fresh ginger
2 Tbsp vegetable oil
1/4 tsp turmeric powder
pinch of chilli powder
2 Tbsp lemon juice
salt to taste
freshly ground black pepper
1 Tbsp crispy fried onion
2 tsp chopped flat-leaf parsley
lemon wedges

In a large saucepan bring 1.5 litres (2 1/2 pints) of water to the boil, add a little salt and boil the beef for 1 hour. Remove and cut the beef into small cubes. Pour half the stock from the saucepan and set aside. Return the beef to the pan and leave over a moderate heat. Meanwhile, chop the shrimps, shallots, garlic and ginger. Heat the oil in a clean saucepan and stir-fry the shrimp, shallot and garlic for 1 minute, then add the ginger, turmeric, chilli powder and reserved stock. Stir well and bring to the boil, then lower heat and allow to simmer for 10 minutes. Next, strain this stock into the saucepan with the meat and continue to cook over a moderate heat for a further 10 minutes. Add the lemon juice, and season to taste with salt and pepper, then bring to a rapid boil. To serve; place a little onion and parsley in the bottom of individual soup bowls and add the meat and the stock. Garnish with lemon wedges.

SOP KAMBING
(soup with lamb or mutton)

450 g (1 lb) lamb or mutton, on bone
1 tsp black peppercorns
2 dried red chillies
1 large onion
2 cloves garlic
salt
2 Tbsp peanut oil
2 Tbsp tamarind water

Garnish:
1 Tbsp fried shallots
2 Tbsp chopped flat-leaf parsley

Trim the fat from the meat and cut into chunks. Crush the peppercorns and chop the chillies. Finely chop the onion and garlic. Place the meat in a large saucepan and add 2 litres (3 1/4 pints) of water. Bring to the boil, add the peppercorns, chillies and 1/2 teaspoon of salt and cook over a moderate heat for 1-1 1/4 hours. Remove the meat with a slotted spoon, allow to cool slightly and cut into small bite-size pieces. Retain the stock. Heat the oil in a clean saucepan and fry the onion and garlic until slightly browned, then add the meat and stir for 2 minutes. Strain the stock into the pan, add the tamarind water and allow to simmer for 30-40 minutes. Adjust seasonings to taste and transfer to a soup tureen. Garnish with the fried shallot and chopped parsley.

Author's Note
Meat cut from the neck or breast is recommended. In Indonesia we particularly like to find, meat still attached to small bones in our soup, that we can pick up in our fingers. The bones also improve the flavour of the stock.

19

Seafoods

PALLU MARA IKAN
(a fish dish from South Sulawesi)

1 fish, or fish steaks, weighing 2 kg
(4 1/2 lbs)
1 tsp turmeric
salt
10 red chillies
8 shallots
3 cloves garlic
20 mm (3/4 inch) knob fresh ginger
375 ml (14 fl oz) tamarind water
2-3 sliced tomatoes

Clean the fish and rub with the turmeric and salt. Seed the chillies and cut lengthwise in half. Slice the shallots, garlic and ginger. Put half the garlic and ginger with half the sliced shallots and five chillies at the bottom of a fish pan and lay the fish on top. Put the remaining chillies, shallots, garlic and ginger on top of the fish, and pour the tamarind water over everything. Add some more salt. Cover the pan and cook slowly for 40-50 minutes. Shake the pan gently from time to time to make sure the fish is not burnt. Add a little more water during cooking if necessary. Remove the fish and allow to cool, then place in the refrigerator overnight. Serve garnished with sliced tomatoes.

Author's Note
Pallu Mara means food that is cooked until all the liquid has evaporated. Use whole or filleted mackerel, or fresh tuna steaks, or any other firm-fleshed white fish.

IKAN RICA-RICA
(grilled fish, Menado style)

1 red snapper, weighing about 1.25
kg (2 1/2 lbs)
1 tsp salt
2 tsp fresh lime juice
4 Tbsp oil
10 shallots
4 cloves garlic
4 fresh red chillies
25 mm (1 inch) knob fresh ginger
4 red tomatoes
1 tsp shrimp paste

Clean and prepare the fish and cut two deep incisions on each side. Rub the fish with the salt, lime juice and half the oil, and set aside in a cool place. Skin the tomatoes, remove the seeds and chop finely. Chop the shallots, garlic, chillies and ginger and place in a blender, together with the shrimp paste, remaining oil and 2 tablespoons of water. Blend until smooth, then transfer to a saucepan and bring to the boil. Boil for 4 minutes, stirring continuously, then add the tomato and continue to stir for a further minute. Adjust the seasonings to taste and remove the pan from the stove. When the paste is cold rub half over the fish, then wrap the fish in foil. Cook in a moderately slow oven (170°C: 325°F: Gas Mark 3) for 45 minutes. Finally, open the foil, spread the remaining paste over the fish and cook under a hot grill for 4-6 minutes. Alternatively, the fish can be grilled throughout on charcoal. When cooked, pour the sauce and the juices from the foil into a bowl. Char the fish on the charcoal for about 4 minutes, turning it over several times. Serve immediately, with the sauce poured over the fish or served separately as a dip.

GARANG ASAM IKAN
(spiced fish steak)

4 fish steaks
1 small onion
1 fresh red chilli
2 cloves garlic
1 small vegetable marrow
2 Tbsp peanut oil
1 tsp crumbled shrimp paste
½ tsp ground galingale
2 Tbsp dark soy sauce
3 Tbsp tamarind water
salt to taste
freshly ground black pepper

Wash the fish and pat dry. Slice the onion, chilli and garlic and cut the marrow into small cubes. Heat the oil in a pan and stir-fry the onion, chilli and garlic for 1 minute then add the shrimp paste, galingale, soy sauce, tamarind water and 250 ml (9 fl oz) of water. Bring to the boil, then lower the heat and allow to simmer for 2 minutes. Add the fish and marrow and season to taste with salt and pepper. Cover the pan and cook over a low heat until the fish is cooked and has soaked up most of the liquid, approximately 30-35 minutes. Remove the fish and serve immediately.

Author's Note
This is a salty, spicy way to cook fish whose meat is rich and compact. It is well suited to fresh tuna and other fish of the same family. It can also be used for steaks of turbot or halibut, monkfish, swordfish and even for the humble dogfish.

PINDANG IKAN
(fish cooked with tamarind)

4 mackerel
225 ml (8 fl oz) vinegar
6 shallots
4 cloves garlic
3 Tbsp vegetable oil
½ tsp chilli powder
½ tsp cayenne pepper
½ tsp ground galingale
1 Tbsp dark soy sauce
4 Tbsp tamarind water
cucumber slices
lemon wedges

Clean and prepare the mackerel and remove the heads. Add the vinegar to 750 ml (1 ¼ pints) of cold water and use to wash the fish, then rinse under cold running water and pat dry. Rub the fish with salt and set aside. Slice the shallots and garlic. Heat the oil in a wok and stir-fry the shallot and garlic for 2 minutes, then add the chilli, pepper, galingale, soy sauce, tamarind water and 500 ml (18 fl oz) of water. Bring to the boil, then lower the heat, adjust seasonings to taste, and allow to simmer for 5 minutes, stirring occasionally. Lay the fish in a casserole dish and pour the sauce on top, then cook in a moderately slow over for 45-50 minutes. Remove the fish and transfer to a serving dish. Strain the sauce over the fish and garnish with the cucumber and lemon wedges.

Author's Note
This is good hot or cold, and it can be eaten as a main dish with rice or as a first course with salad.

IKAN BUMBU ACAR
(red snapper in piquant sauce)

2 medium-size red snappers
2 Tbsp tamarind water
1/2 tsp chilli powder
1 tsp ground coriander
1/2 tsp ground ginger
1 tsp salt
2 cloves garlic

Sauce
flesh of 1 small pineapple
1 red pepper
1 green pepper
2 green chillies
2 shallots
3 candlenuts
2 gloves garlic
1/2 tsp ground turmeric
2 Tbsp vegetable oil
3 Tbsp white vinegar
1/2 tsp dry mustard
salt to taste
1 tsp brown sugar

Clean the fish and cut 2 diagonal slashes on each side. Mix together, in a shallow dish, the tamarind water, chilli, coriander, ginger, garlic and salt. Add the fish, and set aside for at least 1 hour, turning occasionally. Heat the oil in a wok until it is very hot and fry the fish until cooked, approximately 12-15 minutes. Remove and drain off excess oil, then transfer to a serving dish and pour the sauce over the fish.

To make the sauce; cut the pineapple into small cubes, seed and cut the peppers into squares, and seed the chillies. Chop the shallots, candlenuts and garlic and blend together with the turmeric and 3 tablespoons of cold water to produce a smooth paste. Heat the oil in a wok and stir-fry the spice-paste for 1 minute, then add the chillies, vinegar, mustard and salt and 125 ml (4 fl oz) of water. Bring to the boil, then lower the heat and allow to simmer gently for 10 minutes. Add the peppers and continue to cook over a low heat for a further 3 minutes. Finally, add the pineapple and sugar, and stir well.

KARE IKAN
(fish curry)

700 g (1½ lbs) cod fillet
4 shallots
25 mm (1 inch) knob fresh ginger
25 mm (1 inch) knob galingale
25 mm (1 inch) piece lemon grass
3 fresh red chillies
3 candlenuts
1/2 tsp turmeric powder
1/2 tsp salt
600 ml (1 pint) coconut milk

Cut the fish into large bite-size cubes. Chop the shallots. Slice the ginger, galingale and lemon grass and chop the candlenuts. Place all the dry ingredients, excluding the fish, into a blender together with 75 ml (3 fl oz) of the coconut milk. Blend until smooth then transfer to a saucepan, bring to the boil and cook for 4 minutes, stirring continuously. Add the remaining coconut milk and bring back to the boil, then lower the heat and allow to simmer, stirring frequently until the liquid has reduced by half. Next, add the pieces of fish and continue to cook over a moderate heat for a further 8-10 minutes, stirring occasionally. Finally, adjust seasonings to taste and serve immediately.

PEPES IKAN
(marinated fish baked with coconut)

1 kilo (2 ¼ lbs) fish
4 cloves garlic
125 ml (4 fl oz) tamarind water
½ tsp salt
freshly ground black pepper
1 tsp chilli powder
4 Tbsp peanut oil
6 shallots
½ tsp crumbled shrimp paste
1 tsp brown sugar
1 Tbsp fresh lemon juice
125 g (4 oz) freshly grated coconut
2 sprigs fresh mint

If using a large section or steak of fish such as turbot, cut into 4 pieces. Crush half the garlic and mix together with the tamarind water, salt, pepper and half the chilli powder. Pour over the fish and set aside for 30 minutes, turning the fish occasionally. Then, lay the fish, or fish pieces, side by side in a casserole and add the marinade, together with 2 tablespoons of oil. Place in a moderate oven and bake for 25 minutes. Meanwhile, chop the shallots and remaining garlic finely, and crush the shrimp paste with the garlic. Fry in the remaining oil until slightly browned, then add the sugar, lemon juice and remaining chilli powder, and adjust seasonings to taste. Mix well, then add the coconut and 75 ml (3 fl oz) of water. Bring to the boil and allow to simmer for 2-3 minutes. Remove the casserole from the oven, arrange the sprigs of mint on top of the fish and pour on the sauce. Replace the dish in the oven and bake, uncovered, at the same temperature for a further 10-15 minutes. Alternatively, cook under a slow grill until the fish browns on top.

Author's Note
Almost any fish, whole, steaks or fillets, are good for this dish. In Indonesia, Pepes Ikan are wrapped in banana leaves and cooked over a charcoal stove supported on a wire tray, for about 50-60 minutes.

BAKWAN UDANG
(prawn fritters with beansprouts)

175 g (6 oz) prawns
4 spring onions
2 cloves garlic
125 g (4 oz) beansprouts
4 Tbsp rice flour
1 tsp baking powder
3 Tbsp grated coconut
2 Tbsp chopped chives
2 Tbsp chopped parsley
1 tsp ground coriander
1 tsp ground ginger
1/2 tsp chilli powder
2 large eggs
salt and pepper to taste
oil for frying

Shell and de-vein the prawns and chop finely. Slice the spring onions into tiny rounds and crush the garlic. Trim the beansprouts. Place all the above in a mixing bowl and sift in the flour and baking powder. Add the coconut, parsley, coriander, ginger, chilli and 3 tablespoons of cold water, and mix well. Beat the eggs lightly and fold into the mixture. Season to taste with salt and pepper and form into small balls the size of walnuts, then flatten. Heat the oil and deep-fry the patties for approximately 2 minutes, until golden brown. Drain and serve.

UDANG BAKAR
(marinated grilled prawns)

12 king prawns

Marinade:
3 Tbsp light soy sauce
2 Tbsp tamarind water
1 Tbsp peanut oil
1 tsp Sambal Ulek (page 12)
2 cloves crushed garlic
1 tsp brown sugar

Clean the prawns and remove the heads, back shell and black vein. Leave the tails intact. Place the prawns on their backs and slice lengthways halfway through, then lay open and place in a shallow dish. Mix together the soy sauce, tamarind water, peanut oil, sambal ulek, garlic and sugar and pour over the prawns. Ensure all the surfaces are coated, then set aside to marinate for 30-40 minutes. Cook the prawns over charcoal, or under a hot grill for 4 minutes, turning once or twice and brushing occasionally with the marinade.

Author's Note
For this you really need to use the largest king prawns available. The marinade shown here is sufficient for 12-16 king prawns.

UDANG PEDAS MANIS
(hot and sweet prawns)

450 g (1 lb) medium-sized fresh
prawns
½ tsp salt
25 mm (1 inch) piece lemon grass
2 cloves garlic
2 small dried chillies
3 Tbsp palm sugar
2 Tbsp light soy sauce

Remove the heads and legs from the prawns but leave the shells and tails intact. Wash the prawns under cold running water and pat dry, then rub with the salt and set aside in a cool place for 30 minutes. Cut the lemon grass into tiny rounds and crush the garlic and chillies. Pour 125 ml (4 fl oz) of water into a saucepan, add the sugar and bring to the boil. When the sugar has dissolved add the lemon grass, garlic, chilli and soy sauce. Allow to simmer until the liquid has reduced, then add the prawns and stir well to coat evenly. Continue cooking for 3-4 minutes until the prawns are cooked and glazed in the caramelised sauce. Serve hot or cold.

SAMBAL GORENG UDANG
(prawns in rich coconut sauce)

450 g (1 lb) king prawns
2 ripe tomatoes
125 g (4 oz) mangetout
5 shallots
3 cloves garlic
3 candlenuts
1 tsp crumbled shrimp paste
5 red chillies
1 tsp ground ginger
1 tsp ground coriander
a pinch of powdered lemon grass
a pinch of powdered galingale
2 Tbsp vegetable oil
2 Tbsp tamarind water
1 tsp brown sugar
salt to taste
2 kaffir lime leaves
250 ml (9 fl oz) thick coconut milk

Shell and de-vein the prawns. Peel and cut the tomatoes and top and tail the mangetout. Peel and slice the shallots and garlic and pound together in a mortar, along with the candlenuts, shrimp paste and chillies. (Alternatively, blend in a food processor until everything becomes a smooth paste). Transfer into a bowl, and mix in the ginger, coriander, lemon grass and galingale. Heat the oil in a wok, or saucepan, and stir-fry the spice-paste for 2 minutes, then add 250 ml (9 fl oz) of water together with the tamarind water. Add the chopped tomato, sugar, salt and lime leaves and allow to simmer for 8 minutes. Pour in the coconut milk and bring to the boil, then lower the heat and allow to simmer until the sauce is quite thick. Finally, add the prawns and mangetout and cook over a moderate heat for a further 4 minutes, stirring occasionally. Serve with boiled rice.

KEPITING PEDAS
(spicy hot crab)

12 large crab claws
4 Tbsp peanut oil
8 red chillies
2 onions
4 cloves garlic
1 tsp chopped ginger
½ tsp ground coriander
2 Tbsp dark soy sauce
salt
juice of ½ lime

Clean the crab claws and boil them until they turn red (approximately 10 minutes) then fry them in hot oil for 4-5 minutes. Drain, wrap in absorbent paper and keep warm. Reserve the oil. Seed the chillies and slice finely, or crush roughly in a mortar. Peel the onions and garlic and slice finely. Fry the onion and garlic for 2 minutes, stirring continuously, in the reserved oil. Add the chillies, ginger and coriander. Stir and add 3 tablespoons of water, the soy sauce and salt. Simmer for 1-2 minutes, then add the crab claws and lime juice and stir so that the claws are evenly coated. Serve immediately.

Author's Note
This dish can also be made using a whole crab. Clean it and, preferably, take out the brown meat to be used for something else. Chop the body into 4 pieces, and each claw into 2 or 3, then fry the pieces and proceed as described above.

GORENG CUMI-CUMI
(fried squid)

700 g (1 ½ lbs) fresh squid
4 shallots
3 cloves garlic
1 tsp finely-chopped ginger
½ tsp ground turmeric
½ tsp chilli powder
½ tsp salt
1 tsp dark soy sauce
4 Tbsp tamarind water
oil for deep frying

Clean the squid and discard ink sac and heads. Cut the tentacles into 25 mm (1 inch) lengths and slice the body into thin rings. Slice the shallots and crush the garlic, and place in a glass bowl, together with the ginger, turmeric, chilli, salt, soy sauce and tamarind water. Stir well, then add the squid and stir again. Set aside in a cool place for at least 2 hours. Drain and pat the squid dry with kitchen paper. Heat the oil in a wok or deep saucepan, until very hot, then fry the squid in small batches for approximately 3 minutes. Remove with a slotted spoon and serve with rice or vegetables.

CUMI-CUMI ISI
(stuffed squid)

4-6 medium-size squid
2 Tbsp vinegar
125 g (4 oz) chicken breast
3 carrots
3 shallots
1 tsp ground coriander
2 cloves garlic
1 fresh red chilli
salt
freshly ground pepper
3 Tbsp vegetable oil
2 tsp finely chopped ginger
225 ml (8 fl oz) tamarind water
2 Tbsp light soy sauce

Clean the squid and discard the ink sacs and heads. Mix the vinegar in a bowl with 1.2 litres (2 pints) of cold water and add the squid. Leave for 5 minutes, then remove the squid, rinse under cold running water and pat dry. Remove the tentacles and chop finely. Chop the chicken, place in a blender and blend until smooth. Dice the carrots into small pieces and finely slice the shallots, garlic and chilli. Mix the vegetables with the chicken paste, chopped tentacles and coriander and season to taste with salt and pepper. Stuff the mixture into the squid and secure the ends with wooden cocktail sticks. Heat the oil in a frying pan, or wok, and fry the squid, turning frequently, until they are golden brown, then remove with a slotted spoon and drain in a colander. Add the spring onion and ginger to the pan and stir-fry for 1 minute, then add the tamarind water and soy sauce. Allow to simmer for 3-4 minutes and replace the squid. Cover the pan and simmer for a further 5 minutes, adjust seasonings to taste and remove to a serving plate. Slice each squid diagonally into 2 or 3 pieces and serve immediately.

SAMBAL GORENG CUMI-CUMI
(squid in red chilli sauce)

1 kg (2 1/4 lbs) squid
1 Tbsp white vinegar
2 red tomatoes
1/2 tsp sugar
salt to taste

Paste:
6 candlenuts
6-8 red chillies, seeds removed
5 shallots
1 tsp crumbled shrimp paste
2 tsp chopped ginger
a pinch of ground cumin
1 Tbsp chopped lemon grass
3 Tbsp tamarind water
2 Tbsp peanut oil

Clean the squid and discard the ink sacs and heads. Chop the tentacles into 10 mm (1/2 inch) lengths and slice the body into rings. Mix the vinegar with 600 ml (1 pint) of cold water and add the squid. Rinse well, then strain immediately. Peel and chop the tomatoes.

Put all the ingredients for the paste in a blender and blend until smooth. Transfer into a saucepan on a moderate heat and cook, stirring continuously with a wooden spoon, for 3 minutes. Add the tomato, sugar and salt and 250 ml (9 fl oz) of water. Bring to the boil and simmer for a further 4 minutes. Adjust the seasoning and bring the liquid to the boil. Put in the squid, stir, and boil for 3 minutes. Stir again, and serve hot, with rice.

Poultry

AYAM PANGGANG KECAP
(roasted and grilled chicken with soy sauce)

1 medium-size roasting chicken
salt
2 shallots
2 cloves garlic
1/2 tsp chilli powder
2 Tbsp dark soy sauce
2 Tbsp fresh lemon juice
2 tsp peanut oil
2 Tbsp melted butter

Clean and prepare the chicken and rub with salt. Roast in a moderately hot oven until golden brown, then allow to cool and cut into halves. Remove the rib and neck bones and wipe with a kitchen towel, then beat to slightly loosen the fibres of the flesh. Slice the shallots very thinly and crush the garlic, then mix these with the chilli powder, soy sauce, lemon juice and peanut oil. Rub this mixture into the chicken and set aside in a cool place for 1 1/2 hours. Finally, brush the chicken with the melted butter and finish cooking under a hot grill. Serve immediately.

AYAM BETUTU
(chicken with Balinese spices)

6 boned chicken breasts, with skin
salt
350 g (12 oz) curly kale

Spice paste:
5 shallots
2 red chillies
2 cloves garlic
3 candlenuts
2 tsp chopped lemon grass
1 tsp crumbled shrimp paste
2 cloves
1 tsp ground coriander
1 tsp ground cumin
1 tsp ground cinnamon
1/2 tsp ground galingale
1/2 tsp ground nutmeg
1 tsp salt
1/2 tsp white pepper
1 Tbsp fresh lemon juice
2 Tbsp peanut oil

Rub a little salt and half the prepared spice-paste over the chicken and set aside. Blanch the kale, then plunge into cold water. Drain and squeeze out the excess water then chop the leaves and place in a bowl. Add the remaining spice-paste and mix thoroughly, then stuff the mixture evenly under the skin of the chicken breasts. Wrap each breast loosely in 3 layers of aluminium foil and place in a pre-heated oven (150°C: 325°F: Gas Mark 2) for 1 hour, then turn the heat down to 110°C (225°F: Gas Mark 1/2) and continue to cook for a further 1-2 hours. Finally, unwrap and place on a heated serving plate. Serve immediately with rice.

To make the paste; remove the seeds from the chillies. Chop the chillies, shallots, garlic and candlenuts. Place all the ingredients in a blender, add 2 tablespoons of water and blend until smooth. Transfer the paste to a small saucepan and cook over a moderate heat for 5-6 minutes, stirring frequently. Allow to cool before using.

AYAM PANGGANG BUMBU BESENGEK
(roasted and grilled chicken in coconut sauce)

1 chicken, about 1.5 kilos (3¼ lbs)
3 shallots
3 cloves garlic
3 candlenuts
2 tsp chopped lemon grass
½ tsp chilli powder
½ tsp turmeric powder
½ tsp ground coriander
½ tsp ground galingale
2 Tbsp peanut oil
salt to taste
freshly ground black pepper

Cut the chicken lengthwise and discard the rib and neck bones. Wash the halves and pat dry. Slice the shallots, garlic and candlenuts and place in a blender together with the lemon grass, chilli, turmeric, coriander, galingale, peanut oil and 2 tablespoons of water. Blend until smooth, then transfer to a saucepan and bring to the boil. Cook for 3 minutes, stirring frequently, then add the chicken and turn to coat both sides evenly. Pour in the coconut milk and bring to the boil. Cook for 40 minutes, stirring occasionally, then season to taste with salt and pepper and continue to cook for a further 15-20 minutes, until the chicken is tender and the sauce is very thick. Next, remove the chicken and finish cooking over charcoal, or under a hot grill, until slightly charred, then transfer to a serving plate. Finally re-heat the sauce in the pan and pour over the chicken. Serve immediately with rice or boiled potatoes.

AYAM BUMBU ACAR
(chicken in yellow piquant sauce)

4 boneless breasts of chicken
175 g (6 oz) canned bamboo shoots
2 fresh green chillies
3 shallots
3 cloves garlic
3 candlenuts
20 mm (¾ inch) knob fresh ginger
½ tsp turmeric powder
2 Tbsp peanut oil
3 Tbsp white vinegar
1 tsp sugar
1 tsp dry mustard
salt to taste
freshly ground black pepper
2 Tbsp chopped mint

Cut the chicken into bite-size pieces. Slice the bamboo shoots, and seed and slice the chillies. Chop the shallots, garlic, candlenuts and ginger and place in a blender together with the turmeric and peanut oil. Blend until smooth, then transfer to a saucepan and bring to the boil. Stir-fry for 3 minutes, then add the chicken and continue to stir-fry for a further 2 minutes. Next, add the bamboo shoots, chilli, vinegar, sugar and 3 tablespoons of water. Stir, cover the pan and allow to simmer for 3 minutes, then remove the lid, add the mustard and season to taste with salt and pepper. Continue to cook over a moderate heat for 8 minutes, stirring occasionally, then add the mint, stir well, and cook for a final minute. Transfer to a serving dish and serve immediately with boiled rice.

Ayam Goreng Jawa
(fried chicken Javanese style)

1 chicken, about 1.5 kilos (3½ lbs)
5 shallots
3 candlenuts
25 mm (1 inch) stem lemon grass
1 tsp sugar
½ tsp sugar
½ tsp salt
¼ tsp ground galingale
pinch of turmeric
600 ml (1 pint) coconut milk
vegetable oil for deep frying

Clean and prepare the chicken and cut into 8 pieces. Chop the shallots, candlenuts and lemon grass and place in a blender together with the sugar, salt, galingale, turmeric and 75 ml (3 fl oz) of coconut milk. Blend to produce a smooth paste. Pour the remaining coconut milk into a saucepan and place over a moderate heat. Stir in the spice-paste and bring almost to boiling, then add the chicken and cook until all the sauce has been absorbed, approximately 45-55 minutes. Adjust seasonings to taste, then remove chicken and allow to cool. Finally, heat the oil in a wok until it is very hot, then deep-fry the pieces of chicken until golden brown. Serve hot or cold.

AYAM PANIKE
(chicken in aromatic sauce)

1 medium-size chicken
$^1/_2$ tsp salt
vegetable oil for deep frying
6 shallots
4 cloves garlic
4 candlenuts
25 mm (1 inch) knob fresh ginger
1 tsp crumbled shrimp paste
1 tsp chilli powder
2 Tbsp peanut oil
50 mm (2 inch) stem lemon grass
2 kaffir lime leaves
900 ml (1$^1/_2$ pints) coconut milk
1 tsp sugar

Clean and prepare the chicken and cut into 8 pieces, then rub with salt. Heat the vegetable oil in a wok and deep-fry the chicken for 4-5 minutes, then remove, drain off excess oil and set aside. Chop the shallots, garlic, candlenuts and ginger and place in a blender together with the shrimp paste, chilli powder, peanut oil and 3 tablespoons of water. Blend until smooth, then transfer to a saucepan and bring to the boil. Cook for 3 minutes, stirring continuously, then add the chicken and place a lid on the pan. Cook for a further 3 minutes, then uncover, add the lemon grass, lime leaves and coconut milk and bring to the boil. Cook over a moderate heat, stirring frequently, for 40-45 minutes, until the chicken is tender and the sauce is quite thick. Finally, add the sugar, adjust seasonings to taste and stir well. Cook for a further minute, then transfer to a serving dish and serve immediately.

Opor Bebek
(duck in white coconut sauce)

1 duck, about 2 kilos (4 ½ lbs)
10 cm (4 inch) stick rhubarb
4 shallots
4 cloves garlic
4 candlenuts
20 mm (¾ inch) knob fresh ginger
2 tsp chopped lemon grass
1 tsp ground coriander
½ tsp ground galingale
½ tsp chilli powder
2 Tbsp peanut oil
600 ml (1 pint) coconut milk
1 bayleaf
salt to taste
freshly ground black pepper
1 Tbsp melted butter

Roast the duck in a hot oven for 1-1¼ hours until the skin is golden brown. Allow to cool, then cut into halves and remove the rib and neck bones. Cut the rhubarb into short pieces. Chop the shallots, garlic, candlenuts and ginger, and place in a blender together with the lemon grass, coriander, galingale, chilli powder, peanut oil and 3 tablespoons of coconut milk. Blend until smooth, then place in a saucepan and bring to the boil. Cook for 3 minutes, stirring continuously, then add the halves of duck and turn to coat completely with the paste. Add the rhubarb, bayleaf and remaining coconut milk and bring back to the boil. Season with salt and pepper and cook for an hour until the sauce has almost completely reduced. Finally, transfer the duck to an oven proof dish, brush with the melted butter, and place under a hot grill for 4-5 minutes. Serve immediately.

Author's Note
While the duck is cooking in the coconut milk, check at regular intervals to ensure it is not burning or sticking to the pan.

Bebek Hijau
(duck in green chilli sauce)

1 duck, approx. 2 kilos (4 ½ lbs)
4 large fresh green chillies
1 large green pepper
12 shallots
5 cloves garlic
20 mm (¾ inch) knob fresh ginger
¼ tsp turmeric powder
½ tsp ground galingale
2 tsp chopped lemon grass
2 Tbsp vegetable oil
3 Tbsp tamarind water
2 Tbsp chopped chives

Clean and prepare the duck, discard most of the skin, and cut into 8 pieces. Remove seeds from the chillies and pepper. Chop the chillies, pepper, shallots, garlic and ginger, and place in a blender together with the turmeric, galingale, lemon grass, vegetable oil and tamarind water. Blend until smooth, then transfer to a large saucepan and bring to the boil. Cook for 3-4 minutes, stirring continuously, then add the duck and continue stirring for a further 2 minutes. Season to taste with salt and pepper, and add the lime leaves and 450ml (16 fl oz) of water. Bring back to the boil, then cover the pan, lower heat and allow to simmer for 1 hour. Next, remove the cover and increase the heat. Allow to boil rapidly for 10 minutes until the stock has reduced considerably, then remove from the heat and allow to cool. Store for at least 12 hours in the refrigerator, then skim off the fat and place back on the stove. When the duck is thoroughly re-heated add the chives and stir for a further minute before transferring to a serving dish.

Sate

Sate Daging, Sate Kambing, Sate Ayam (beef, lamb and chicken satays)

450g (1lb) rump steak
450g (1lb) lean meat from leg or
shoulder of lamb
2 large chicken breasts
2 chicken thighs

Marinade:
6 shallots
2 cloves garlic
1 tsp finely-chopped ginger
2 tsp ground coriander
1 tsp chilli powder
¹/₂ tsp salt
2 Tbsp malt vinegar
4 Tbsp light soy sauce
4 Tbsp peanut oil

Cut the meat into 20 mm (³/₄ inch) cubes and place in the prepared marinade. Leave for at least 2 hours (or overnight in the refrigerator), then thread onto wooden skewers and grill over red-hot charcoal for 4-5 minutes, turning frequently. Serve with Lontong (see page 64) and Sambal Kacang (see page 12).

To make the marinade, slice the shallots very finely and chop the garlic. Place all the ingredients in a large bowl and mix thoroughly.

Author's Note
Sate is, I suppose, the one classic Indonesian dish that everyone knows. This recipe will serve 8-10 people. For those people who don't like peanut sauce, it is a quick and easy matter to make up a bowl of Sambal Kecap instead (see page 12).

Meats

KALIO and RENDANG
(traditional Sumatran beef dishes)

1.5 kg (3½ lbs) brisket
6 shallots
3 cloves garlic
2 tsp ground ginger
1 tsp turmeric
3 tsp chilli powder
25 mm (1 inch) knob galingale
1.75 litres (3 pints) thick coconut milk
1 bayleaf
1 stem lemon grass
1 tsp salt

KALIO

Cut the meat into largish (about 30 mm: 1¼ inch) cubes, bigger than bite-sized. Peel and finely slice the shallots and crush the garlic. Put these, with all the other ingredients (except the meat) into a large wok. Then put the meat in, give it a stir, and start cooking over a medium heat. Let it bubble for 2½ hours, stirring it from time to time. The coconut milk will have become quite thick by the end of this time. Finally, adjust seasonings to taste and serve hot, with plenty of rice.

RENDANG

To make Rendang, transfer the Kalio to a clean wok and continue cooking over a low heat for another 30 minutes, still stirring occasionally. (There will now be more oil in the wok and the sauce will be thicker and darker). Stir continuously for a further 15-20 minutes, or until the oil has almost disappeared.

Author's Note
Kalio and Rendang are, in effect, the same dish. The only difference is that you stop cooking Kalio when there is still quite a lot of the rich golden sauce left in the pan.

BESENGEK DAGING
(boiled silverside in spicy sauce)

450g (1lb) silverside
1 onion
2 Tbsp vegetable oil
1 Tsp crumbled shrimp paste
½ tsp ground turmeric
1 tsp ground coriander
¼ tsp chilli powder
¼ tsp sugar
salt to taste
2 Tbsp tamarind water
300ml (10 fl oz) thick coconut milk

Boil the meat for 1 hour, then allow to cool and slice. Retain 225ml (8 fl oz) of the cooking stock. Slice the onion. Heat the oil in a wok, add the onion and shrimp paste and stir-fry for 1 minute. Then, add the turmeric, coriander, chilli, sugar, salt and tamarind water and stir well. Add the meat and the reserved stock and bring to the boil. Cover the pan and cook over a moderate heat for 5 minutes, then remove the cover and pour in the coconut milk. Bring back almost to the boil, then lower the heat and cook for approximately 30 minutes, stirring occasionally, until the sauce becomes thick. Serve immediately.

Semur Daging Dengan Kentang
(beef and potatoes in soy sauce)

2 sirloin or fillet steaks
1 large potato
2 shallots
1 clove garlic
2 Tbsp butter
2 very thin slices of ginger
2 Tbsp dark soy sauce
$1/4$ tsp ground white pepper
a large pinch ground nutmeg
1 large tomato
3 spring onions
2 hard-boiled eggs

Cut the steaks into 4 pieces and slice the potato. Finely chop the shallots and garlic, peel and chop the tomato and cut the spring onions into tiny rounds. Heat the butter in a large frying pan, add the shallots, garlic and ginger and stir-fry for 2 minutes, then add the potato and continue to cook for 4 minutes, stirring frequently. Add the meat and cook for 2 minutes on each side, then add the soy sauce, hard-boiled eggs, pepper and nutmeg and cover the pan. Cook over a moderate heat for 4 minutes, then remove the cover, add the tomato and spring onion and adjust the seasonings to taste. Cover the pan again, increase the heat and cook for a further minute. Transfer to a serving plate and cut hard boiled eggs into halves.

Author's Note
If you prefer, you can use sliced boiled beef, but this is a quick recipe using sirloin or fillet steaks. Use more potatoes if you are going to serve it without rice or pasta. Then you will only need salad to accompany it.

Empal
(boiled and fried silverside of beef)

1 kg (2 lb 3 oz) silverside of beef
$1/2$ tsp salt
3 fresh red chillies
3 cloves garlic
1 tsp ground coriander
$1/4$ tsp ground galingale
1 tsp sugar
1 Tbsp tamarind water
300 ml (10 fl oz) thick coconut milk
vegetable oil for frying

Put the piece of beef into a large saucepan and add sufficient cold water to cover. Add the salt and bring to the boil. Cook for 2 hours by which time there should be about 250 ml (9 fl oz) of stock remaining. Remove the beef from the pan and cut into 8-10 slices. Flatten these slightly with a meat hammer. Remove the seeds from the chillies and crush the garlic. Bring the stock in the pan back to the boil, add the chillies, garlic, coriander, galingale, sugar, tamarind water and coconut milk and replace the meat. Then, lower the heat, adjust seasonings to taste and allow to simmer until most of the stock has been absorbed. Set aside to cool, then heat the oil in a frying pan and fry the slices of meat for 2-3 minutes. Serve immediately with rice, or allow to cool and serve with a salad.

DENDENG RAGI
(a dry beef dish, cooked in grated coconut)

225 g (8 oz) topside of beef
3 shallots
2 cloves garlic
1 tsp chilli powder
1 tsp ground coriander
½ tsp ground galingale
1 tsp brown sugar
2 Tbsp tamarind water
2 kaffir lime leaves
225 g (8 oz) freshly-grated coconut
1 Tbsp peanut oil

Cut the meat into small, thin squares and place in a wok. Slice the shallots and crush the garlic, and add to the meat, together with the chilli, coriander, galingale, sugar, tamarind water and lime leaves. Pour in 450 ml (16 fl oz) of water and bring to the boil. Place a lid on the wok and cook for 40-45 minutes, then uncover and add the coconut. Stir well and allow to simmer until the liquid has been absorbed, then stir again thoroughly, add the oil and continue to stir-fry until the coconut is golden brown. Serve hot or allow to cool and serve as a side dish.

Author's Note
Dendeng Ragi can be stored in an airtight container for a few days, then stir-fried to reheat.

DENDENG BALADO
(braised beef with chilli)

500 g (1 lb 2 oz) rumpsteak
2 Tbsp tamarind water
½ tsp salt
¼ tsp freshly-ground black pepper
4 Tbsp peanut oil
2 cloves garlic
2 onions
2 red chillies
¼ tsp salt
1 tsp sugar

Cut the meat into thin slices, and marinate well in the tamarind water seasoned with salt and black pepper. Leave in a cool place for at least 20 minutes. Crush the garlic and slice the onions and chillies.

Heat the oil in a frying pan, and fry the slices of meat, in batches, for about 3 minutes on each side, turning them over once. Remove the meat and drain on absorbent paper. Then, in the same frying pan, stir-fry the garlic, onion and chillies for 3 minutes. Season with salt and sugar, and pour in 2 tablespoons of water. Bring to the boil and put the meat back into the pan. Cover and simmer for 3-4 minutes, then uncover, increase the heat and cook on a high heat until all the liquid has disappeared. Adjust seasonings to taste, and serve hot with rice or noodles.

DAGING BUMBU BALI
(beef cooked in chilli and tamarind sauce)

350 g (12 oz) roast beef
3 shallots
2 cloves garlic
2 large red chillies
1 tsp chopped ginger
1 tsp crumbled shrimp paste
1 Tbsp dark soy sauce
4 Tbsp tamarind water
2 Tbsp peanut oil
salt and pepper to taste

Slice the beef, finely chop the shallots, garlic and chillies. Heat the oil in a wok, or frying pan and fry the shallots, garlic and chillies for 3-4 minutes, then stir in the ginger, shrimp paste, soy sauce and tamarind water. Add the beef together with 125 ml (4 fl oz) of hot water, and season with salt and pepper. Continue cooking over a low heat for 5-8 minutes. (The mixture must not go dry, but the sauce should be very thick). Finally adjust seasonings to taste and serve hot with vegetables and rice, noodles or pasta.

Author's Note
This is a good way to use leftovers of roast beef.

SAMBAL GORENG HATI
(calf's liver in coconut sauce)

450 g (1 lb) calf's liver
100 g (4 oz) mangetout
2 ripe tomatoes
1 large onion
4 fresh red chillies
3 cloves garlic
3 candlenuts
1 tsp chopped ginger
1 tsp chopped lemon grass
1 tsp crumbled shrimp paste
1 tsp paprika
1 tsp ground coriander
large pinch ground galingale
2 Tbsp tamarind water
2 Tbsp peanut oil
600 ml (1 pint) coconut milk
2 kaffir lime leaves
salt to taste

Cut the liver into small bite-size pieces. Top and tail the mangetout. Peel and chop the tomatoes. Chop the onion, chillies, garlic and candlenuts and place in a blender together with the ginger, lemon grass, shrimp paste, paprika, coriander, galingale, tamarind water and peanut oil. Blend until smooth. Transfer to a saucepan and bring to the boil. Allow to simmer, stirring frequently, then add the coconut milk and bring almost to the boil. Stir well and allow to simmer until the liquid has reduced by half, then add the mangetout, tomato and lime leaves. Bring back to the boil and stir in the liver. Continue to cook, stirring continuously for 2 minutes, then add salt to taste and serve immediately.

MARTABAK
(stuffed savoury pancakes)

Casing:
120 g (4 oz) won ton skins
75 ml (3 fl oz) corn oil

Filling:
450 g (1 lb) minced lamb or beef
2 large onions
2 cloves garlic
1 Tbsp vegetable oil
1 tsp ground coriander
1/2 tsp ground cumin
1 tsp ground ginger
1 tsp chilli powder
1/2 tsp turmeric
1 Tbsp finely chopped lemon grass
4 spring onions
3 eggs

Cut the onion into thin slices and crush the garlic. Chop the spring onions and set aside. Heat 1 tablespoon of oil in a wok and fry the onion and garlic until soft, then add the coriander, cumin, ginger, chilli, turmeric and lemon grass and stir to mix thoroughly. Fry for a further 30 seconds, stirring continuously, and add the meat. Mix well and cook for 15 minutes, stirring occasionally. Allow to cool for 45 minutes then transfer the mixture to a bowl and add the spring onions. Beat the eggs, season with a little salt and add to the bowl. Mix thoroughly. Lay half the won ton skins on a pastry board and put 1 tablespoon of the mixture onto each skin. Place another skin on top and press the edges to seal. Heat the oil in a heavy-based frying pan to a high temperature, and fry the martabaks, pressing them down with a spatula, for approximately 2 minutes on each side, turning once. Drain on absorbent paper and serve hot.

Author's Note
The casing should be quite crisp around the edges but not in the middle, and the finished martabak should be flat and evenly filled with meat almost to the edge.

KAMBING ASAM PEDAS
(hot and sour lamb)

500 g (1 lb 2 oz) lean lamb
1 tsp salt
4 shallots
2 cloves garlic
1 tsp chopped ginger
4 candlenuts
3 Tbsp tamarind water
1 tsp ground coriander
1/2 tsp chilli powder
1 tsp paprika
2 large red or yellow peppers
120 ml (4 fl oz) vegetable oil

Cut the meat into thin slices, then cut these diagonally into bite-sized pieces. Place in a bowl, and rub well with the salt. Set aside in a cool place. Chop the shallots, garlic and candlenuts and blend together with the ginger, coriander, chilli, paprika and tamarind water to produce a smooth paste. Remove seeds, then cut the peppers into diamond-shaped pieces. Heat the oil in a wok, or large saucepan, and fry the meat in batches for 3 minutes. Remove each batch with a slotted spoon and lay the meat on absorbent paper to drain. Discard all but 2 tablespoons of the oil and, in this, fry the spice-paste for 3 minutes, stirring continuously. Replace the meat and continue stirring for 2 minutes, then add the peppers and 100 ml (4 fl oz) of hot water. Stir well and cook for a further 2 minutes. Finally, adjust seasonings to taste and serve with rice or pasta.

KAMBING BUMBU BACEM
(spicy boiled lamb)

To serve 8-10 people

1 shoulder of lamb, about 1.5 kg
(3 1/2 lbs)
1 large onion, peeled and sliced
5 cloves garlic, crushed
1/2 - 1 tsp chilli powder
2 tsp brown sugar
1 Tbsp tamarind pulp
2 tsp ground coriander
1 tsp chopped ginger
large pinch of ground galingale
1 kaffir lime leaf
salt

Place the meat in a deep saucepan. Slice the onion and crush the garlic, and add these to the pan. Add sufficient cold water to cover the meat and bring to the boil. Add the remaining ingredients, lower the heat slightly and cook at a gentle boil for 1 3/4-2 hours. Then take out the meat, allow to cool and cut it into good large slices. Put these in another saucepan, and strain over them the stock from the first pan. Adjust seasonings to taste and cook over a high heat until the sauce has been reduced to half its original quantity. Serve immediately.

GULE KAMBING
(lamb stew)

1 kg (2¼ lbs) shoulder of lamb
1 onion
2 cloves garlic
4 candlenuts
1 Tbsp chopped lemon grass
1 tsp finely chopped ginger
⅓ tsp chilli powder
⅓ tsp cayenne pepper
⅓ tsp ground galingale
½ tsp turmeric
120 ml (4 fl oz) tamarind water
900 ml (1½ pints) thick coconut milk

1 Tbsp vegetable oil
1 tsp brown sugar
2 tsp ground coriander
3 cloves
1 bay-leaf
small stick of cinnamon
salt to taste

Bone the lamb and cut into small pieces. Chop the onion and garlic and put in a blender together with the candlenuts, lemon grass, ginger, chilli powder, cayenne pepper, galingale, turmeric and tamarind water. Blend for a short time to produce a smooth paste. Heat the oil in a saucepan and fry the spice-paste for 1 minute then add the meat and stir-fry for 2 minutes. Next, add 450 ml (16 fl oz) of water and bring to a low boil. Cover the pan and allow to simmer for 15 minutes, then uncover and add the sugar, coriander, cloves, bay leaf, cinnamon stick and coconut milk. Stir well and bring just to boiling point, then lower heat and allow to simmer for 25-30 minutes, stirring frequently. (At the end of this time the sauce will have reduced by half.) Remove the cloves, bay leaf and cinnamon stick and adjust seasonings to taste. Serve immediately.

Author's Note
This is a liquid lamb stew - or you can think of it as a very meaty soup. Do not use flour to thicken the sauce. The best way to eat gule is to put some boiled rice in a soup plate, ladle the gule over it, and eat it with a spoon.

GULAI KAMBING DENGAN REBUNG
(lamb stew with bamboo shoots)

450 g (1 lb) lean leg of lamb
170 g (6 oz) canned bamboo shoots
3 shallots
2 cloves garlic
2 Tbsp peanut oil
2 tsp ground coriander
½ tsp chilli powder
½ tsp turmeric
1 tsp chopped ginger
2 kaffir lime leaves
900 ml (1½ pints) coconut milk
salt

Cut the lamb into small, thin strips and slice the bamboo shoots. Slice the shallots and garlic very finely. In a saucepan, fry the shallots in the oil for 2 minutes, then add the garlic, coriander, chilli powder, turmeric, ginger and kaffir lime leaves. Stir-fry these for 2 minutes and add the meat. Continue stirring for 2-3 minutes, pour in the coconut milk and add the bamboo shoots. Bring the liquid just to boiling point, stir, and simmer gently for 35-40 minutes. By the end of this time the sauce will have been reduced considerably, but it should still be quite runny, not thick. Adjust seasonings to taste, and serve hot with rice and vegetables.

BABI KECAP
(pork cooked in soy sauce)

500 g (1 lb 2 oz) fillet of pork
1 Tbsp light soy sauce
2 Tbsp plain flour
125 g (4 oz) button mushrooms
4 cloves garlic
25 mm (1 inch) knob fresh ginger
3 Tbsp dark soy sauce
pinch of chilli powder
2 Tbsp rice wine
2 tsp lemon juice
6 Tbsp vegetable oil

Cut the pork into small cubes. Put the flour into a bowl and add the light soy sauce, mixing well together. Coat the pork with the mixture and let it stand for at least 30 minutes. Clean and slice the mushrooms. Peel the garlic and ginger and slice thinly. Heat the oil in a wok or heavy-based frying pan, and fry the meat, in two batches, for 4 minutes, turning it occasionally . Discard all but 2 tablespoons of oil, leaving any of the flour-coating from the meat in the bottom of the pan. Reheat and fry the garlic, ginger and mushrooms, stirring continuously, for 1 minute. Add the soy sauce, 2 tablespoons of water and replace the meat. Mix well, season with the chilli powder, and stir-fry continuously for 1-2 minutes. Just before serving, add the rice wine and the lemon juice. Stir and serve immediately.

Author's Note
If freezing, do not add the wine and lemon juice at the time of cooking. To serve from the freezer thaw the meat out completely and heat quickly on a high flame for 2-3 minutes, stirring or shaking the pan well all the time. Add the wine and lemon juice just before serving.

SEMUR BABI DENGAN BIHUN
(pork and vermicelli in soy sauce)

500 g (1 lb 2 oz) tenderloin of pork
4 Tbsp transparent vermicelli
2 shallots, finely chopped
1 clove garlic, finely chopped
1 large tomato, peeled and chopped
3 spring onions, cut into thin rounds
2 Tbsp butter
2 very thin slices of ginger
2 Tbsp dark soy sauce
1/4 tsp ground white pepper
a large pinch of ground nutmeg

Cut the meat into thin slices. Put the vermicelli into a bowl and pour over sufficient warm water to cover it. Put a lid on the bowl and leave the vermicelli to soak for 4 minutes, then drain and cut several times across so that the strands are not too long. Rinse under the cold tap, and keep in a colander till needed. Finely chop the shallots and garlic, peel and chop the tomatoes and cut the spring onions into tiny rounds. Heat the butter in a large frying pan, add the shallots, garlic and ginger, and stir continuously for 2 minutes. Add the meat and cook for 2 minutes each side, turning once, then add the soy sauce, pepper and nutmeg. Cover the pan, and cook over a moderate heat for 4 minutes. Uncover, adjust seasonings to taste, and add the tomatoes, spring onions and vermicelli. Cover the pan again, and turn up the heat for a further minute. Uncover, stir to mix thoroughly, then transfer to a shallow plate and serve immediately.

Author's Note
Bihun is transparent vermicelli made from mung beans. It is widely available in the west, from oriental grocery shops.

BABI ASAM PEDAS
(hot and sour pork)

450 g (1 lb) lean fillet of pork
1 tsp salt
75 ml (3 fl oz) malt vinegar
175 g (6 oz) canned bamboo shoots
4 shallots
2 cloves garlic
1 tsp chopped ginger
3 candlenuts
125 ml (4 fl oz) sunflower oil
1 tsp chilli powder
1 Tbsp sugar
3 Tbsp chopped mint or sweet basil

Cut the meat into small pieces and place in a bowl. Rub the salt and 2 teaspoons of vinegar into the meat and set aside in a cool place. Drain the bamboo shoots. Blend the shallots, garlic, ginger, candlenuts and chilli powder with 2 tablespoons of the oil and 2 tablespoons of water to produce a smooth paste. Heat the remaining oil in a frying pan, or wok, and fry the pieces of pork in batches for 4 minutes each. Remove with a slotted spoon and drain on absorbent paper. Discard all but 2 tablespoons of the oil. Reheat and fry the paste for 3 minutes, stirring continuously. Then add the sugar and remaining vinegar. Stir, add the pork, bamboo shoots and 4 tablespoons of water and bring to the boil. Lower heat and allow to simmer for 2 minutes, then adjust seasonings to taste. Cook for a further minute, then add the chopped basil and stir well. Serve immediately with rice or boiled new potatoes.

Vegetables

GADO GADO
(mixed vegetable salad with peanut sauce)

125 g (4 oz) cabbage
125 g (4 oz) French beans
125 g (4 oz) carrots
125 g (4 oz) cauliflower
125 g (4 oz) beansprouts
1 medium-size potato
1/4 cucumber
1 hard-boiled egg
150 ml (5 fl oz) Sambal Kacang
(see page 12)
2 Tbsp crispy fried onion
2 prawn crackers

Clean and prepare the vegetables. Shred the cabbage, slice the beans and carrots and break the cauliflower into florets. Boil the vegetables separately; the cabbage, beans, carrots and cauliflower for 3-4 minutes, the beansprouts for 2 minutes and the potato for 15 minutes. Allow the potato to cool, then remove and discard the skin and cut into slices. Slice the cucumber and the hard-boiled egg. To serve; arrange the beansprouts in the middle of a serving plate, surround with the cabbage, beans, carrots and cauliflower and top with slices of potato and egg. Heat the sauce and pour it over the salad and finally garnish with crispy-fried onions and prawn crackers.

Author's Note
You don't have to worry too much about keeping the vegetables hot as Gado Gado is best eaten lukewarm.

ASINAN JAKARTA
(crunchy vegetable and fruit salad)

125 g (4 oz) white cabbage
125 g (4 oz) Chinese cabbage
1 cucumber
2 medium-size carrots
2 apples
2 hard pears
225 g (8 oz) beansprouts

Dressing:
3 Tbsp palm sugar
5 bird peppers
1 fresh red chilli
125 g (4 oz) roasted peanuts
2 Tbsp dried shrimps
1/2 tsp crumbled shrimp paste
1 Tbsp caster sugar
2 tsp salt
225 ml (8 fl oz) malt vinegar

Wash and prepare the vegetables and fruit. Shred the cabbage, cut the cucumber and carrots into medium-size sticks and slice the apples and pears. Place in the salad bowl containing the dressing and toss well to ensure an even coating.

To make the dressing; melt the palm sugar in a saucepan together with 2 tablespoons of water. Slice the bird peppers and chilli and blend together with the peanuts, dried shrimps, shrimp paste, caster sugar, salt and vinegar, to produce a coarse paste. Transfer the paste to a bowl, add the palm sugar syrup and adjust seasoning to taste. Mix well.

URAP
(vegetable salad with coconut dressing)

125 g (4 oz) Chinese cabbage
2 large carrots
6 radishes
1 small cucumber
1 spring onion
75 g (3 oz) beansprouts
1 Tbsp chopped mint

Dressing:
1 tsp crumbled shrimp paste
1 clove garlic
$1/2$ tsp chilli powder
$1/2$ tsp sugar
salt to taste
2 Tbsp fresh lime juice
75 g (3 oz) freshly-grated coconut

Shred the cabbage, cut the carrots into thin sticks, slice the radishes and cucumber and chop the spring onion. Place in the salad bowl containing the prepared dressing, add the beansprouts and mint and toss to mix thoroughly.

To make the dressing; place the shrimp paste in a salad bowl and crush with the back of a spoon. Crush the garlic and add to the bowl, together with the chilli powder, sugar and salt. Mix, then add the coconut and lime juice and mix again thoroughly.

TERIK BUNCIS
(French beans in candlenut sauce)

450 g (1 lb) French beans
4 shallots
4 candlenuts
2 cloves garlic
1 tsp crumbled shrimp paste
2 Tbsp vegetable oil
1 tsp ground coriander
$1/2$ tsp ground cumin
$1/2$ tsp chilli powder
1 tsp salt
1 kaffir lime leaf
225 ml (8 fl oz) coconut milk

Top and tail the beans and cut into 10 mm ($1/2$ inch) pieces. Chop the shallots, candlenuts and garlic and blend together with the shrimp paste, oil and 2 tablespoons of water to produce a smooth paste. Transfer the paste to a saucepan, add the coriander, cumin, chilli powder, lime leaf and coconut milk and bring to the boil. Stir and let the sauce simmer until reduced by half, then add the beans and season with salt. Cook over a moderate heat for 6 minutes, then transfer to a dish and serve immediately.

OSENG-OSENG CAMPUR
(stir-fried mixed vegetables)

3 medium-size carrots
175 g (6 oz) yard-long beans
125 g (4 oz) cauliflower florets
75 g (3 oz) beansprouts
3 shallots
2 Tbsp peanut oil
1 tsp crumbled shrimp paste
1/4 tsp chilli powder
1 tsp dark soy sauce
salt to taste
freshly ground black pepper

Cut the carrots into sticks, about 35mm (1¹/₂ inches) long and cut the beans to the same lengths. Trim the beansprouts and slice the shallots thinly. Heat the oil in a wok or large frying pan, and stir-fry the shallot for 2 minutes, then add the shrimp paste, chilli powder and soy sauce. Mash the shrimp paste slightly with a wooden spoon. Add the carrots and beans and stir-fry for 3 minutes, then add the cauliflower and continue to stir-fry over a high heat for a further 3 minutes. Pour in 125 ml (4 fl oz) of water and bring to the boil, then add the beansprouts. Cover the pan, lower the heat and allow to simmer for 2 minutes. Finally, uncover, add seasonings to taste and, if necessary to avoid vegetables burning, a little more water. Continue to cook for 2-3 minutes, stirring continuously, then serve immediately.

TUMIS BAYEM
(stir-fried spinach)

450 g (1 lb) spinach
2 shallots
2 cloves garlic
1 green or red chilli, seeds removed
2 Tbsp peanut oil
1 tsp chopped ginger
2 Tbsp light soy sauce
salt to taste

Discard the stalks of the spinach and wash the leaves thoroughly. Slice the shallots, garlic and chilli very finely. Heat the oil in a wok, or saucepan, and fry the shallots, garlic and chilli for 1 minute, then add the ginger and spinach and continue to cook for another minute, stirring continuously. Next cover the pan and cook over a moderate heat for a further minute, then uncover and add the soy sauce and salt to taste. Continue stirring for a final minute before serving.

TERANCAM
(raw vegetables and tempeh with coconut dressing)

225 g (8 oz) tempeh (see Glossary)
125 g (4 oz) yard-long beans
3 spring onions
1 medium-size cucumber
1 fresh red chilli
125 g (4 oz) beansprouts
2 bird peppers
1 clove garlic
1 tsp shrimp paste
225 g (8 oz) freshly-grated coconut
1 tsp sugar
1 tsp salt
2 Tbsp fresh lime juice
3 Tbsp chopped sweet basil

Quarter the slab of tempeh and grill for 4 minutes on each side. Leave to cool, then slice into small thin squares. Wash the beans and spring onions and slice into thin rounds. Cut the cucumber into quarters lengthways, scoop out the seeds and cut into thin slices. Cut the chilli into thin rounds and wash the beansprouts. Place all the above in a salad bowl. Crush the peppers, garlic and shrimp paste and mix with the coconut, sugar, salt and lime juice. Add the mixture to the salad bowl together with the sweet basil and toss to mix thoroughly.

Acar Campur
(mixed cooked vegetables in yellow piquant sauce)

175 g (6 oz) French beans
175 g (6 oz) carrots
175 g (6 oz) cauliflower florets
8-10 small pickling onions
2 shallots
2 cloves garlic
3 candlenuts
1 large fresh chilli
1/2 tsp ground turmeric
2 Tbsp distilled white vinegar
2 Tbsp peanut oil
salt
1 tsp mustard powder
1 tsp sugar
freshly ground black pepper

Top and tail the beans and cut each into 2 or 3 pieces. Cut the carrots into sticks of a similar length. Chop the shallots, garlic, candlenuts and chilli and place in a blender, together with the turmeric, vinegar, peanut oil and 1/2 teaspoon of salt. Blend until smooth, then transfer to a wok and bring to the boil. Boil for 4 minutes, stirring continuously, then pour in 125 ml (4 fl oz) of water and bring back to the boil. Add the onions, stir, and cover the wok. Cook for 2 minutes, then add the beans and carrots and continue to cook for 3 minutes. Next add the cauliflower, mustard and sugar, lower the heat, and simmer for a further 3 minutes. Finally, uncover the pan, adjust seasonings to taste and turn the vegetables over a few times. Serve hot, or allow to cool and store in the refrigerator.

Author's Note
Acar (pronounced atjar) is a generic term in many Eastern countries for a vegetable or mixed-vegetable dish, raw or cooked, lightly pickled with vinegar, and mildly or not-so-mildly spiced.

Goreng Terong
(fried aubergines)

2 medium-size aubergines
salt
1 large onion
250 ml (9 fl oz) vegetable oil
1 tsp paprika
1/2 tsp chilli powder
1/2 tsp sugar

Cut the aubergines, crossways, into 3 pieces, then quarter each piece. Place in a colander and sprinkle a little salt over all the cut surfaces. Set aside for 30 minutes, then wash and pat dry with kitchen paper. Slice the onions thinly. Heat the oil in a wok and fry the aubergine in batches for 3-4 minutes, turning frequently, then remove and drain. Discard all but 2 tablespoons of the oil. Reheat the remaining oil and stir-fry the onions for 2 minutes, then add the paprika, chilli powder and sugar and continue to stir-fry for a further minute. Finally, add a little salt, replace the aubergine and stir for a few seconds before serving.

Rice & Noodles

NASI KEBULI
(savoury rice with chicken)

450 g (1 lb) long-grain rice
4 shallots
2 cloves garlic
50 mm (2 inch) stem lemon grass
2 tsp ground coriander
1/2 tsp ground cumin
pinch of ground galingale
pinch of ground nutmeg
10 mm (1/2) inch stick cinnamon
2 cloves
1/2 tsp salt
1 roasting chicken
oil for deep frying

Garnish:
1 Tbsp crispy-fried onion
1 tsp chopped parsley
1 tsp finely-sliced chives
cucumber slices

Soak the rice in cold water for 1 hour. Chop the shallots, garlic and lemon grass and mix with the coriander, cumin, galingale, nutmeg, cinnamon, cloves and salt. Prepare the chicken, cut into serving size pieces and pack in a saucepan together with the spice mixture. Add just sufficient cold water to cover the chicken and bring to the boil. Cook until the chicken is tender, approximately 40-45 minutes. Meanwhile, strain the rice and wash it several times in cold water, then drain thoroughly. Heat a tablespoon of oil in a saucepan and stir-fry the rice for 5 minutes. Strain off the stock from the chicken and add 600 ml (1 pint) to the rice. (If there is insufficient stock, make up the quantity with hot water.) Bring to the boil and cook until all the liquid has been absorbed, then transfer the rice to a steamer and steam for 10 minutes. At the same time heat the remaining oil in a wok and deep-fry the chicken for 3-4 minutes until the skin is golden and crispy. To serve; arrange the rice in the centre of a large serving plate, surround with pieces of chicken and garnish with the crispy-fried onion, parsley, chives and cucumber slices.

LONTONG
(compressed rice)

225 g (8 oz) long-grain rice
1/2 tsp salt
banana leaves or muslin

Wash and drain the rice. Pour 2 litres (3 1/2 pints) of water into a saucepan and bring to the boil. Add the bags of rice and allow to simmer for 1 1/4 hours, adding more boiling water as necessary to keep the rice covered. (The rice will expand to fill the bags and the grains will then be compressed to form a solid mass.) Drain in a colander and allow to cool, then refrigerate until required. To serve, cut open and strip off the banana leaf, or cloth, and cut the rice into large chunks.

To prepare the bags, cut the banana leaves into 15 cm (6 inch) squares. Roll each piece to make a cylinder and close one end, securing it with a cocktail stick. Fill one-third full with the rice and close and secure the other end. If using cloth cut and sew into bags 15 cm (6 inches) square, fill one-third with rice and stitch to close. In either case there must be plenty of room for the rice to expand.

NASI GORENG
(fried rice)

450 g (1 lb) long-grain rice
3 shallots
2 fresh red chillies
1 clove garlic
125 g (4 oz) button mushrooms
125 g (4 oz) pork or chicken
1 Tbsp butter
1 Tbsp paprika
½ tsp paprika
½ tsp chilli powder
1 Tbsp light soy sauce
2 tsp tomato puree
salt to taste

Boil the rice in 600 ml (1 pint) of water then set aside for 2 hours. Finely slice the shallots and chillies and crush the garlic. Slice the mushrooms and chop the meat into small pieces. Heat the butter in a wok and stir-fry the shallots, chillies and garlic for 1-2 minutes, then add the mushroom and meat and continue to cook for 2 minutes. Add the paprika, chilli powder, soy sauce, tomato puree and salt and stir well. Cook for a further 1-2 minutes, then add the rice and stir continuously until the rice is hot. Adjust seasonings to taste and transfer to a serving plate. Garnish with slices of tomato and cucumber and crispy-fried onion.

NASI PUTIH
(plain boiled and steamed rice)

450 g (1lb) long-grain rice
600 ml (1 pint) water

Wash and drain the rice, then place in a heavy-based saucepan and add the water. Bring to the boil and allow to simmer until all the water has been absorbed, approximately 12-15 minutes. Place a tightly-fitting lid on the pan and turn the heat down as low as possible. Leave the rice to cook for 10-12 minutes, then remove from the heat and allow to rest (still covered) for a further 5 minutes. Alternatively, when the first stage of boiling has been completed and the water has been absorbed, transfer the rice to a steamer or double saucepan and steam for 12-15 minutes.

Author's Note
In Indonesia, we do not use any salt in boiling or steaming plain rice.

NASI KUNING
(yellow savoury rice)

450 g (1 lb) long-grain rice
2 Tbsp vegetable oil
1 tsp turmeric powder
1 tsp ground coriander
1/2 tsp ground cumin
600 ml (1 pint) coconut milk
1/2 tsp salt
50 mm (2 inch) cinnamon stick
1 clove
1 bayleaf

Soak the rice in cold water for 1 hour, then wash and drain in a colander. Heat the oil in a saucepan, add the rice and stir-fry for 2 minutes. Add the turmeric, coriander and cumin and continue to stir-fry for a further 2 minutes. Then pour in the coconut milk, add the salt, cinnamon stick, clove and bayleaf and bring to the boil. Cook until the liquid has been absorbed, then steam the rice for 10 minutes. Alternatively, after boiling place a tightly-fitting lid on the pan and leave over a low heat for 10 minutes, then remove from the heat and allow to stand for a further 8-10 minutes. Discard the cinnamon stick, clove and bayleaf before serving.

NASI UDUK
(coconut rice)

450 g (1 lb) long-grain rice,
2 Tbsp peanut oil
600 ml (1 pint) coconut milk
1 tsp salt
pandanus leaf or bayleaf

Soak the rice in cold water for 1 hour, then wash under cold running water and drain thoroughly. Heat the oil in a saucepan and stir-fry the rice for 3 minutes, then add the coconut milk, salt and pandanus leaf (or bayleaf) and boil until all the liquid has been absorbed. Finally, cover the pan with a tightly-fitting lid and leave, undisturbed, over a low heat for 12-15 minutes. Discard the pandanus leaf (or bayleaf) before serving.

Alternatively, when the first stage of boiling has been completed and the coconut milk has been absorbed, transfer the rice to a steamer, or double saucepan, and steam for 12-15 minutes.

MIE REBUS
(noodles in soup)

225 g (8 oz) egg noodles
90 g (3 oz) topside of beef
3 shallots
2 cabbage leaves
2 carrots
1 tsp ground coriander
1 tsp chopped ginger
2 Tbsp light soy sauce
1.2 litres (2 pints) beef stock
4 spring onions
1 large tomato
salt and pepper
2 Tbsp vegetable oil

Put the noodles in salted boiling water and boil for 3 minutes (or according to the instructions on the packet). Turn out of the saucepan into a colander and hold under running cold water for a few seconds, then leave to drain. Cut the beef into small pieces. Slice the shallots finely. Peel and slice the carrots, and shred the cabbage coarsely. Clean and chop the spring onions. Peel, seed and chop the tomato. Heat the oil in a wok and fry the shallots for one minute. Add the coriander and ginger. Stir for a few seconds, then add the beef and stir-fry for a few minutes. Add the carrots and cabbage, and continue stirring for about 2 minutes. Add the soy sauce and stock and simmer for 8-10 minutes. Next add the noodles, chopped tomato, spring onions, salt and pepper. Increase the heat, and cook for a further 1-2 minutes. Adjust seasonings to taste and serve hot.

Author's note
Chicken may be substituted for the beef, in which case use a chicken stock.

BAKMIE GORENG
(savoury fried noodles)

225 g (8 oz) egg noodles
100 g (4 oz) topside of beef or pork
fillet
75 g (3 oz) shrimps
5 shallots
2 cloves garlic
4 spring onions
2 tomatoes
2 cabbage leaves
100 g (4 oz) beansprouts
2 medium-size carrots
vegetable oil
3 tsp soy sauce
salt and pepper to taste
flat-leaf parsley

Put the noodles into salted boiling water and boil for 3 minutes (or according to the instructions on the packet). Turn them out into a colander and wash under cold running water for a few seconds, then drain. Cut the meat into small pieces. Shell and de-vein the shrimps. Slice the shallots finely, crush the garlic and chop the spring onions. Seed and chop the tomatoes and shred the cabbage. Trim the beansprouts, dice the carrots and roughly chop the parsley. Heat the oil in a wok and stir-fry the shallot for 1 minute, then add the garlic and meat. Continue stir-frying for 2 minutes, then add the cabbage and carrots, and continue stir-frying for about 4 minutes. Add the shrimps, noodles and beansprouts and continue stir-frying for 3 minutes, then add the soy sauce, chopped tomatoes and spring onions. Adjust seasonings to taste and continue frying until the noodles are really hot. Garnish with parsley and serve immediately.

MIEHUN GORENG
(fried rice vermicelli)

225 g (8 oz) rice noodles
2 Tbsp vegetable oil
5 shallots
1 tsp ground coriander
1 tsp finely-chopped ginger
2 cabbage leaves
2 carrots
2 skinless chicken breasts
3 spring onions
2 tomatoes
120 g (4 oz) cooked peeled shrimps
1 Tbsp light soy sauce
salt and pepper to taste

Put the vermicelli into a saucepan, and pour in boiling water to cover it. Cover the pan and leave to stand for 3 minutes (or according to the instructions on the packet). Turn the vermicelli out of the pan into a colander, and hold it under running cold water for a few seconds, then leave it to drain. Slice the shallots finely, peel and slice the carrots, and shred the cabbage leaves coarsely. Slice the chicken breast into small, thin pieces. Clean and chop the spring onions. Peel, seed and chop the tomatoes. In a wok, heat the oil, and fry the shallots for 1 minute, then add the ground coriander and ginger. Stir for a few seconds, add the chicken pieces, carrots and cabbage, and continue stirring for about 5 minutes. Add the soy sauce and vermicelli and go on stirring for 3 minutes. Next add the chopped tomatoes, spring onions, soy sauce and shrimps. Turn and stir for 1 minute, adjust seasonings to taste and continue stirring for a further 1-2 minutes. Serve immediately.

Desserts

LAPIS LEGIT
(cinnamon layer cake)

450 g (1 lb) unsalted butter
1 tsp vanilla essence
225 g (8 oz) caster sugar
16 egg yolks
3 Tbsp top of milk
150 g (5 oz) plain flour
1.5 Tbsp ground cinnamon
1 tsp ground cloves
2 tsp grated nutmeg
pinch of salt
8 egg-whites

In a large mixing bowl, beat the butter, vanilla and half the sugar until creamy. In another bowl, beat the egg yolks with the remaining sugar until thick and creamy, then pour into the original bowl. Add the milk and stir to combine well, then sift in the flour, spices and salt and fold in carefully. Beat the egg-whites until stiff and fold these into the batter mixture. Butter the base of a 23 cm (9 inch) square, loose-bottomed cake tin and pour in a thin layer of batter, approximately 3 mm (1/8 inch) thick. Place this under a very hot grill (if using an oven grill, pre-heat the oven to 150°C (300°F: Gas Mark 2) then turn it off before switching on the grill) for approximately 2 minutes until the batter has set firm, then pour on another layer of batter and grill in the same way. Continue until all the batter has been used up, then place in the oven (pre-heated as above) and leave for 10 minutes. Turn out on to a wire rack and allow to cool, then slice thinly and cut into pieces about 50 mm (2 inches) square.

Author's Note
While an oven with a grill inside is ideal, the cake can be cooked under an ordinary grill and finished off in the oven. A good Lapis Legit will consist of at least 12-14 layers and will keep moist and fresh in a cake tin, or, wrapped in aluminium foil, in the fridge for at least a week. It can also be frozen.

PUTU AYU
(steamed coconut cup-cake)

5 eggs
4 Tbsp caster sugar
125 g (4 oz) rice flour
4 Tbsp plain flour
pinch of salt
150 ml (5 fl oz) thick coconut milk
125 g (4 oz) freshly-grated coconut

Beat the eggs and sugar until thick and creamy. Add the flour and salt, then slowly pour in the coconut milk, beating continuously. Beat the batter for a further 3 minutes. Divide the grated coconut into 10 or 12 small cups and press down firmly. Boil water in a steamer and place the cups inside to warm the coconut, then top up each cup with the batter and steam for a further 10 minutes. Allow to cool slightly, then turn out on to a wire rack. Serve warm or cold.

KUE LABU
(pumpkin cake)

350 g (12 oz) peeled pumpkin
125 ml (4 fl oz) coconut milk
pinch of salt
2 eggs
3 Tbsp brown sugar
4 Tbsp rice flour
1/2 tsp ground cinnamon
1/4 tsp grated nutmeg
1 Tbsp melted butter

Cut the pumpkin into cubes and place in a saucepan together with the milk and salt. Cook over a low heat until the pumpkin is tender, then transfer to a bowl and mash with a fork. Beat the eggs and sugar for 2-3 minutes, then add to the pumpkin. Sift in the flour, add the cinnamon, nutmeg and butter and mix thoroughly. Pour the mixture into a well-greased 23 cm (9 inch) square cake tin and bake in a pre-heated, moderate oven for 30-35 minutes. Turn out and serve warm or cold.

Author's Note
This cake is not supposed to rise very much, but if you want to make it lighter use a teaspoon of baking powder.

NAGASARI
(rice flour cake with banana)

2 large ripe bananas
125 g (4 oz) rice flour
2 Tbsp corn flour
pinch of salt
1 litre (1 3/4 pints) coconut milk
4 Tbsp granulated sugar

Slice the bananas into rounds, about 10 mm (1/2 inch) thick. Sift the rice flour, corn flour and salt into a bowl and slowly add 225 ml (8 fl oz) of water, stirring continuously with a wooden spoon to produce a smooth, runny batter. Pour the coconut milk into a saucepan, place over a moderate heat and bring almost to the boil. Slowly pour in the batter and, stirring continuously, cook over the same moderate heat for 15 minutes, then add the sugar and continue to stir for a further 10 minutes. For the next stage of cooking, pour sufficient batter into small ramekins so that they are three-quarters full, then top with a slice or two of banana. Cover each ramekin with foil and place, side by side, in a large saucepan. Pour boiling water into the pan to come half-way up the sides of the cups, then place a tightly-fitting lid on the pan. Finally, bring the water back to the boil and allow to simmer for 10 minutes. Serve hot or cold.

KOLAK LABU
(pumpkin in coconut syrup)

450 g (1 lb) pumpkin flesh
225 g (8 oz) desiccated coconut
90 g (3 oz) brown sugar
salt
1 cinnamon stick

Peel and cut the pumpkin into 4 or 8 pieces. Put the desiccated coconut in a liquidizer with 600 ml (1 pint) of recently-boiled water. Liquidize for a few seconds, then sieve the milk, squeezing the desiccated coconut until it is really dry. Put the coconut back into the liquidizer, add another 600 ml (1 pint) of water and repeat the process, but do not mix with the first, thicker, coconut milk. Discard the dry coconut flakes. Put the thin coconut milk in a saucepan with the pumpkin pieces, add a pinch of salt and boil for about 8 minutes. Drain off the milk, but leave the pumpkin in the saucepan. In another saucepan, bring the thick coconut milk slowly to the boil, with the brown sugar, cinnamon stick and a pinch of salt. When it starts to boil, stir continuously for about 3 minutes, taste, add more sugar if desired, and pour this syrup into the pan with the pumpkin, discarding the cinnamon. Simmer for 1 or 2 minutes. Serve hot or cold.

RUJAK
(spicy fruit salad)

1 pomelo
1/2 cucumber
1 small pineapple
2 hard apples
1 large half-ripe mango
1 small yam bean

Sauce:
2 hot chillies
1/2 tsp crumbled shrimp paste
175 g (6 oz) palm sugar
1/4 tsp salt
2 Tbsp fresh lemon juice

Segment the pomelo and wash and peel the fruit as required. Slice the cucumber and cut the remaining fruit into bite-size pieces. Arrange in a bowl and pour the sauce on top. Stir well to ensure all the fruit is coated with the sauce.

To make the sauce; chop the chillies and pound, together with the shrimp paste, sugar and salt, until smooth. Add the lemon juice and stir well.

Author's Note
For this, hard, half-ripe fruit are usually best, certainly better than ones that are too soft. The idea of the dish is that the bumbu, the sauce, should be not only spicy but also sweet enough to sweeten the crunchy fruit. Note that if the apple and pineapple are being prepared in advance they should be placed in slightly-salted water and drained immediately prior to serving.

Glossary

BAMBOO SHOOTS
Buy canned ones - fresh ones are not worth the trouble. Young shoots, packed in glass jars, are nice, but not necessary. The ones in cans may be in big chunks, or sliced.

CANDLENUTS
In Indonesia we call these kemiri. You can buy them in oriental food shops, but failing that, use macadamia nuts. Don't pop raw candlenuts into your mouth - they are mildly toxic until cooked.

CHILLIES
You can now buy both fresh and dried chillies easily in Britain. Dried chillies should be soaked in warm water for 5-10 minutes before use. The bigger the chilli, the less hot it is and, in the hot chillies, the really 'fierce' part is the seeds. In these recipes, therefore, I advise you to remove the seeds, unless you are used to chillies and like very spicy food. The juice of chillies can irritate the skin, and especially the eyes. Rub a little salt on your hands before you cut into a chilli, and wash your hands afterwards. Keep your hands away from your face and eyes.

COCONUT MILK
If you use freshly-grated coconut flesh, one nut will make about 600ml (1 pint) of standard-thickness milk. Pour hot water over the grated flesh and let stand till lukewarm. Then squeeze the flesh in handfuls to extract the milk, and finally sieve it. For thick milk, use less water.

If you use desiccated coconut, a 170g (6-oz) pack will make 600 ml (1 pint) of thick milk or twice this quantity of standard milk. Put the coconut in a blender and pour over it half the water, hand-hot. Run the blender for 20-30 seconds. Pass the mush through a fine sieve, pressing and squeezing to extract the maximum liquid. Put the coconut back in the blender and repeat the process. The milk can be stored in the fridge for 24 hours, but it cannot be frozen. If you intend to freeze a dish, leave out the coconut milk and only add it when the dish has been thawed ready for re-heating. (Rendang and Kalio, however, can be frozen, because the milk has been more or less completely absorbed into the meat.)

DRIED SHRIMPS (or dried prawns)
These small shrimps or prawns, roasted and packed in plastic bags, can be bought at oriental food shops. Soak in cold water for 10 minutes before use, then chop, crush or blend with other ingredients.

FLAT-LEAF PARSLEY
This is also called, in Britain, continental or Chinese parsley. The leaves look like coriander, but are quite flat. Celery leaves are a good substitute.

GALINGALE (also galangal; Indonesian, laos, Thai, ka)
In the shop, this looks something like root ginger, but pinker, and tastes different. Powdered galingale is also obtainable.

GINGER
When I started writing cookbooks, I had to use powdered ginger in most recipes. This has very little taste and fresh ginger, now readily available, should be used whenever possible. It may be chopped or sliced and used as a separate ingredient in the cooking or finely chopped and blended with other spices to produce a paste.

KAFFIR LIME LEAF
This is one of several leaves that we use to give a pleasant aroma to savoury dishes; salam leaf is another. These are obtainable in Britain, but bay leaf, though not the same, produces a similar effect.

NOODLES

There are three types you are likely to find in the shops and in this book: **egg noodles** (mie or mee), made of wheat flour and eggs and sold in rectangular blocks like contorted spaghetti. Some Chinese shops sell fresh ones, but the dried ones are as good and keep for months; **rice vermicelli** (miehun), very thin strands of what looks like fine wire. Rice sticks are thicker, looking like narrow white ribbon; **bean threads** (biehun), very thin strands, colourless and almost transparent, made from mung beans; also called cellophane noodles or glass noodles.

PALM SUGAR

A hard, brown sugar, made from the juice of the coconut palm flower, and sold in solid cakes; you chip bits off and crush it. Sometimes sold under its Anglo-Burmese name, jaggery.

PANDANUS LEAF

You can buy these long, narrow leaves in oriental shops, in packets; they are used to give aroma and colour. For aroma, put a piece of leaf in the pan, during cooking, and remove before serving. For colour, liquidize a leaf or two in a little water, then strain.

RED ONIONS

When shallots are out of season, you can still find these imported little red onions in Chinese and Thai shops.

SHRIMP PASTE (Indonesian, terasi or trassie; also blachen, balachan)

This is a fermented shrimp paste, extremely pungent and salty; it is used in very small amounts, but it is quite easy to find in oriental shops (in Thai shops, ask for kapi) and there is no substitute for it, as you will realise when you smell it. But don't be put off by the smell; the result of adding it to your cooking is delicious. It is sold either in blocks of about 200g, or in small slices of about 5g, in plastic packs. If you buy a large block, slice it about 5mm (1/4 inch) thick, spread the slices on a sheet of aluminium foil, fold this over and seal the edges to make a flat parcel, and roast in a medium oven for 10 minutes. When cool, store in an airtight jar. The little 5g pieces have already been roasted or grilled.

TAMARIND AND TAMARIND WATER

Tamarind, in Britain, is usually sold in blocks of dried pulp. To make tamarind water, cut a chunk from the block and simmer it in water for several minutes. Let it cool, then squeeze and strain it to extract the juices and flavour. Discard the remnants of the pulp, pips etc. Tamarind water looks like old washing-up water, but don't be put of by this; it tastes good and doesn't affect the appearance of the dish.

TEMPEH (Indonesian, tempe)

This is often described as "cultured soybean cake". Soya beans are packed with vitamins, proteins etc. but are largely indigestible by humans. Soy sauce and tofu are partial solutions to this problem, but only tempeh keeps the whole beans intact, with all their fibre. The beans are cultured with a fungus which digests the parts humans can't digest, binds the beans together and has a faint but pleasantly nutty flavour of its own. Fresh or frozen tempeh, made in Holland or Britain, can now be found in many health food shops. It is an ideal food for vegans, but anyone can enjoy it.

WONTON WRAPPERS

These are very thin pastry squares, sold in packets in Chinese shops, usually by weight. They are about 7.5cm (3 inches) square. They must be bought either fresh or frozen; in the fridge they keep only a few days. They need to be moist and flexible when you use them, so keep them well wrapped up. If you freeze a large quantity, split them into small individually-wrapped packs, and thaw them thoroughly before use.

Index